Soulmate Warrior
by Bette Regennia Rinker

RoseDog 🐾 Books
PITTSBURGH, PENNSYLVANIA 15222

ISBN: 978-0-8059-8929-8

Printed in the United States of America

First Printing

For more information or to order additional books, please contact:
RoseDog Books
701 Smithfield Street
Third Floor
Pittsburgh, Pennsylvania 15222
U.S.A.
1-800-834-1803
www.rosedogbookstore.com

CHAPTER 1

MY BEST GOOD FRIEND

❦❦

Kelsie called to ask me to meet her at K-Bob's Steak House. It's located right off the freeway in our little town of Truth or Consequences. I don't even remember the drive there as I was about ready to jump out of my skin with joy as I had something to share with my "best good friend" that I knew she would love to hear. It seemed that my car just pulled into the usual spot, from memory I suppose. I do remember getting out of my car, not even closing the door all the way shut, kind of skipping up on the sidewalk and then into the restaurant.

I knew one didn't have to look hard to find Kelsie anywhere she was. She was, she truly was my best and many other people's, "best good friend", as Forest Gump portrayed in the movie. She had a love for life that anywhere she was, it radiated out of her entire being. The kind of love that comes from deep inside her, better known as the soul, I suppose.

Yes, there she was in the favorite corner we always ask for, so we could take our break from our beauty shops without too much interference and then we could set about trying to solve the little and big problems that would come our way once in a while.

Kelsie motioned for me to hurry and sit down and tell her the news as quickly as I could get it out. We managed to look up and see the waitress kind of pushing us along to get with the program. If she hadn't been a new waitress, she would have already known what we wanted. Just about every day we ordered the same dish of huevos rancheros and two steaming hot coffees. Now!....we thought we could sit here and work on our problems as long as it took. Needless to say, we probably shouldn't have taken that table so many times and for so long. We're sorry K-Bobs, for treating your restaurant as though it was our second home and we are also grateful.

Through it all, I could hear Kelsie insisting I hurry and blurt out the good news that I had told her over the phone, I would share with her. I took a deep breath, tried to settle my thoughts so that Kelsie would understand what on earth was going on that was so different from anything else I had ever told her. I looked at Kelsie's bright happy face. I was so happy that she was happy and it became truly important to me to tell Kelsie and to reveal to you this true, and wonderfully great story as clearly as I understood it. But, more than that, it became really important to me that I explain it in a way that what was happening to me, if Kelsie wanted it and asked for it, positively could have this unspeakable joy. I am confident you can have it too just for the asking and believing; the way we show our belief, we may be asked to go through some earth shaking changes. My mind was racing now!...Where should I begin?

I hadn't even mentioned these people to Kelsie before, with the exception to tell her some nice people had volunteered to drop me off at the El Paso, Texas bus station in May. That was so, I could attend my musician's son's wedding in Austin. I wonder now, why I trusted them to take me so far away as over a hundred miles, when I usually don't accept a ride to town, which is just ten blocks away. Trust is the key word here, and to meet Lara was to love her and trust her. Let me tell you a little about her.

CHAPTER 2

LARA

⫸⫷

Lara, I thought and everyone that saw her would comment that she looked like Loretta Lynn; and she believed that I looked like Dolly Parton and especially sounded like her. I knew Dolly had always said she would have been a hairdresser if she had not chosen to sing country music. I'd always loved Dolly and considered it a compliment when people would mistake me for her. I told Lara, that Dolly and I were from the same neck of the woods in the South. Lara would come and get her hair fixed about twice a month. We had people come up to us to sign autographs for them as they had mistaken us for these stars. So we would laugh and say someday we would travel around the United States as look a likes; that way we could travel in style and enjoy this great country as though we were actually them. Then, we decided that wouldn't be fair as we had not done their kind of homework and we were sure it was monumental.

Kelsie and I were the kind of girls that loved our families, our church, our friends and especially our little town of Truth or Consequences. My son, John Christian, wrote a commercial for it that sings, "everybody here will be your friend, so, snowbirds when are you going to fly back in?" That's because you that are from the extremes winter weather lands, come here to escape the ravaging cold of winter. We are like the "best kept secret" in the world: And it is so true, that it does take a village to make a feeling of completeness in a family. To make a beautiful completed tapestry, every strand brings to it, its own beauty. The color, the design tells a story that means something a little different to each of us, but makes us realize we're just as important as anything to the design of the whole picture. Just try leaving a little piece of the puzzle out of the picture and it will drive you just as crazy as leaving a big piece of the puzzle out of the picture. Many people are driven to find that piece of their heart. To some of us, it becomes the driving force in our lives. Somewhere in there, we begin to believe, nothing belongs to us. When in reality, I learned, you know what, it all belongs to us!!!! I think, my first son Joe, taught me that. I couldn't realize why he didn't have to own anything. Why he was so at peace with just what he had, and that was his family and friends. Until this sunk in, I searched feverishly for that piece of the puzzle that would connect it all for me, and the ones I cared about. That's why I'm writing this long letter to you. I just wanted to tell you to hang in there. It's a wonderful and surprising ending. It's like we start out thinking like this:

I thought of age and loneliness and change
I thought how strange we grow when we're alone
And how unlike the selves that met and talked
And flipped the switch and said, "Goodnight"
Alone, the word is endured and known
It is the stillness where our spirit walks
And all but in most faith is overthrown.

Poems I had written in my youth were racing through my mind now. I don't know if I even remember them right as I had long since put them away. I, also, had long since tucked away with them somewhere in the chamber of my heart, something that I realized was important to complete; but I wasn't driven now. I was settled into other fun hobbies and projects. Anything I felt would bring more joy to others.

I missed seeing Lara; and I thought his name was Beryl, her husband. I had cut their hair often enough that I would wonder where they were if they hadn't shown up at least once or twice a month for their hair work, or to show their company the old dresser in my shop that belonged to Beryl's grandfather years ago. They were amazed that I would pick it out and buy it from one of the local antique dealers.

And what puzzled them more, I had also picked out another one that had belonged to Mr. Hamilton a little later in the Walk-a Bout antique store just across the street from my first beauty shop on the broadway of our little town.

They are still on display in my own "Steel Magnolias" beauty shop. Have you ever been drawn to something you just had to have? Lara was so intrigued by that.

One day, I turned around in my shop while cutting someone's hair and there was Lara and her daughter Kathy. I was so happy that her daughter had come to visit her for a while as Lara would call me a few times and tell me how unhappy she was with moving away from them. She sounded so alone and I would wonder where her husband was and think to myself, that no one should feel that alone with a mate in their lives. But honestly, I didn't think too far into it as I had many clients who had extreme health problems. I couldn't afford to worry, as I would get down myself. So, I would try to just send Lara happy thoughts and how very much I cared for her well being; we both were newcomers to Truth or Consequences at that time. Later on I found out her husband was taking care of their business in another town. He said.

I told Kelsie about the time I had to go and check on Lara when she told me she didn't think she was going to make it. She had called the shop several times to change her appointment in one day, each time she would set her appointment a little later in the day. She never did make it! So, I took my rollers and hair paraphernalia and started walking to her house to check on her. When I got there, the door was a little a jar and I heard her beloved dog Sweet Pea barking. She was a Jack Russell terrier and had a fierce bark. I thought she was huge, but when I finally got to meet her she was a little lap dog and loved to cuddle. I banged on every door. I can remember now as I stood there what an eerie feeling came over me. I finally gave up and walked back home. Again, I tried to let it go and not worry. I really didn't know what to worry about.

Lara finally called a few nights later just to ask me if I was happy in Truth or Consequences. I assured her that I loved it here! She said she was really sorry that she had moved here. She missed Austin and being around her family. I told her, I thought, we owe it to ourselves and to them to be as happy as we can be in any situation life throws at us. Little did I know the emotional and physical pain she must have been in. I was going to learn soon. That was the last time I talked with Lara or was ever to see her again. I was pretty bitter. How could she just give up? How could she just go away, just as my Mother had when I was four? Now, that I think back I realized that Lara reminded me of my Mother in so many ways. She had the same dark hair; she was tall and slim, almost too slim and as far as I know one didn't see either of them smile that much. There seemed to be a longing in them that they believed would never cease. I remember thinking how beautiful they would be if they would only become conscious of what they have and smile about it. It seemed I just turned around and Lara was gone for good.

I couldn't help but wonder what it would have taken to make them sit up straight, breath deep and just smile, just because they were chosen to get to visit planet Earth.

CHAPTER 3

INTRODUCTION TO BERYL

❧❧

One day I was out watering shrubbery for my landlord Stedmond Byron, who by the way was buying up the whole town little by little. Someone pulled into the yard and said, "Hello." I asked him to come on in as I recognized him as Lara's husband. I asked him his name again, of course I was embarrassed, I never could get his name. I had never heard it in the south, especially not in the mountains of "Ole Kentucky". You know they would have laughed at that name there, so I just never registered it. Each time I saw him, I always believed it was the last. In the end, I was right. I found out that he was just not the kind of guy to stick around. I learned Lara was with him for years, but only because she didn't marry him. They did finally marry, after years of living together, but she didn't enjoy that marriage long and she should have. She was one of the most deserving people you will ever meet. It's then, that you realize they were so perfect they seemed to be ready to meet their maker and continue on the eternal process that never ends.

I'm looking forward to seeing her again, along with my Mother and loved ones and the people who have worked hard on behalf of my spirit. I know there are people you can say that about also. It's like a breath of fresh air or a spring flower to get to meet someone like that. I often wonder when we get to heaven, if we'll ask people for their autographs. Those are the true autographs to get excited about!!!!!!!

It was a flashback as Kelsie and I were sipping our now cold coffee, so cold that Kelsie ordered a large tea to go with it and she reached all the way across the long table and shook my arm, almost screaming now so loud that most of the restaurant on our side could hear her say, "Regennia, Regennia, go on and tell me. What's going on?"

"Well", I told Kelsie, after learning of Lara's passing, I felt really bad for Beryl. I would see him sometimes when I was walking my dog, Rusty. He would pull over and tell me he was considering suing the hospital for his wife's death. He would have a lot of papers as though he was working on it. Then, when you and I and John moved me into my new home; he was the man who helped without complaint. I saw him also when I attended the church across the street from my new home. Well it was built in the fifties, but it had been remodeled, so it was new to me. It was a beautiful older home and was worth way more than what I bought it for. I wondered, many times in the future, if that had attracted Beryl to me more than yours truly.

Beryl was in my church now and, alone. He just seemed to be the perfect gentleman. After church, he would always ask if I needed a ride home. I was happy to have the company, as it was the first time in my life that I had been without family around me. He would come in and sit across the room and sometimes cry for the loss of Lara; I just wanted to hold him and tell him everything would be alright as Lara was home now and had a beautiful family to carry on her affairs.

Soon, he came into the shop and told me he was moving his daughter out here from Virginia to live with him. I remember being somewhat relieved that he would have some company and I wouldn't have to worry about him again. Beryl gets things done fast. So, before I knew it, she was moved in and had pretty much taken over Beryl's life. I couldn't help remember the comment that Lara had made about being afraid they were too close. I told Beryl about her comment one night and he laughed and said that the doctors had her so drugged up, that she was saying a lot of things all over town; but not to worry, it was just the medicine talking. I was so relieved.

So night after night, I sat and listened to this guy talk, before I realized who he was.

CHAPTER 4

DAWNING OF A SOULMATE

❦

"Kelsie, this is my 'soulmate'!" The guy I had been looking for all my life. I learned in those talks that we came into this world together; him first, me second, a few months later. At this entrance here on earth, our Mother's, Maud and Ruia, gave us the same initials. My mother died when I was four, soon after that and I was sent to a missionary school and literally raised by them. Beryl's mother became a missionary when her two boys were raised and much of Beryl's family was prayer warriors. I so admired that. We both had a very rocky world, but I attributed that to us not being able to find one another. It seemed though that all we really wanted was to serve the Lord. That was our dream. I want to tell you that he didn't look anything like I thought I was looking for and he didn't fit my idea at all of a soulmate. I had always been drawn to the tall, dark and handsome guy with plenty of charisma. Beryl, I came to learn was just a quiet little man about my own size, his hair was grayed, but there was a beautiful light that radiated out of his eyes when we were together. I loved that light. I always gave Lara the credit for the light in Beryl's eyes for one simple reason; when I met them, they were trying so hard to be born again Christians.

But now, as I sat and listened to him from across the room, it dawned on me slowly that maybe this was the part of my heart that was missing and had been missing all of my life. I know that is a tall order for anyone!!! I accept that. I wish that I could find that artist that made for me that beautiful wooden heart with soft warm curves that had a large hole in the middle where he had placed a beautiful, dancing, full of fire, opal. This artist presented that heart to me in a restaurant one coffee morning as a surprise and looked me in the eyes and simply said, "I know what you mean when you say soulmate." The wood grains represent the things we pad with; the fire opal represents the missing link. "Oh no", I told the artist "I can't just take this beautiful heart without paying for it." He looked at me and said, "Pass it on." And he just disappeared. I never did see him again but you can bet, I still take very seriously my debt of passing it on.

On one of these coffee morning's, still, on the cool coast of highway one, I was sitting in a rugged, old restaurant that faced the ocean and smelled of fresh fish. I met a young, almost albino man, I never knew his name. He came over to my table; he asked if he too could enjoy the beautiful view. It was the same table I always occupied for my morning coffee and reveries as I peered at the timeless horizon where the ocean and sky would meet in the distance. He poured out his heart about his girlfriend having an abortion and killing their baby. He was totally torn apart. I tried telling him our soul truly has a match and how I believed it worked. I told him one didn't have to own, control or possess that soulmate in order to be happy, but to merely allow that essence one admired of your soulmate to reflect from you also…Kind of by osmosis, you become what you love and respect. His tears stopped as he listened but I believed that he was, yet, too fragile to leave on his own. Truthfully, I didn't know what to do, so I took my beloved redwood/beryl, fire opal heart out of my purse and presented it to him. He too, said he couldn't take it and I said the same thing the un-named artist said to me, "just pass it on". Keep it as long as you need it, and when you meet someone who needs it worse than you, give it away. I'd love to see the path that heart took.

Somehow always my mind goes back to those events. But today I had forgotten; I was totally consumed with finding out what this guy Beryl meant when he said he had feelings for me and was interested in being with me forever.

"Oh great" said Kelsie. "This is wonderful news." It reminds me of a movie I just recently saw where this guy gave this girl a ring and asked her to be with him forever. She replied, "Sure, and forever begins this moment." They then gave one another a warm, passionate kiss as you might have guessed. Kelsie added in her excitement, "Let's go tell Beryl right now."

We, finally, relinquished our table, tipped the waitress well and headed for Beryl's house. In this way, I guess we did put the rush on him. I knew in my heart that it didn't matter to me because I had actually been waiting for years, from the time I became cognizant of someone being there for me. I think I was eight or nine when I became so sure. Beryl seemed to be waiting for us even though we had not called. He seemed to be very happy to see us. I turned to Kelsie and asked her to tell him why we were there. Kelsie told Beryl the story. Beryl agreed with us. He gave us a big hug with that beautiful smile I loved. He agreed that was the way it was and said he would take care of the papers and appointments at the courthouse. We left like little children who had just caught a glimpse of heaven.

CHAPTER 5

THE SOULMATE RINGS

✺✺

It really wasn't long before Beryl called and said he would like to take me to Las Cruces to shop for our rings. It's about seventy five miles there, but we turned up the radio real loud and sang old time religious songs all the way there. Our hands were sweating, and we would steal quick kisses so as not to distract Beryl from the highway. It felt like waking up from a blanket of sleep and the hearts had finally decided it would be alright to peer out from under that blanket of protection as though winter was over and we were now headed for springtime. We ended up at Sam's Club for some reason. We walked straight up to the jewelry counter and sure enough there was the ring that represented my soulmate path. Beryl's daughter had told me that he had worried all night that I wouldn't get what I wanted. She added to be sure to pick out a nice one as he wanted only the best for his love...

The ring I went right up to reminded me why I would never give up on my soulmate path. How could it be so perfect?????? The diamonds were arranged like the vision was that happened years ago in my beauty shop in Paradise, California where I would always go to pray everyday. I was about to say the Lord's Prayer; my head was bowed and my eyes were closed when there appeared in front of me an old man with bright piercing, blue eyes and long gray hair and a beard, almost to his waist... I was so shocked I started batting my eyes, to come back from wherever I had gone in that flash of a moment. The grayed haired man could see I was petrified, so he just glided over to the other side of the shop. He had a staff in his hands, which he used to point to a bubbly pool of golden essence. I figured out that was his way of telling me that he did not need oxygen and could break through time. At the time the staff hit the golden essence, something shot through me like a bolt of energy. I would go everyday hoping to see him again, until I realized his appearance was forever in my heart.

Again, my mind flashed back to the time Beryl and Lara volunteered to take me to the El Paso bus station. I remember, I got on the bus at night-fall and slept all night. Some lady that had gotten on with me in El Paso, kept on talking; all I could hear her say was, "Well, I sure wish I could sleep that easy." It was the kind of a sleep one enjoys as a child. The rolling wheels making its own kind of music, sort of a lullaby. I tuned into the soothing hum rather than the ladies whining, irritating vocals that was little more than demanding. The last thing I remembered before I fell asleep was the irritation in her voice with me that I didn't have time for her messed up life; not realizing at all, that mine was just like hers. All messed up, but each of us was literally going somewhere.

At that time though, my life seemed to be blissfully peaceful. My children were raised now, and for the first time in my life, I was free to do exactly as I pleased. I felt like jumping out of my skin. That's as happy as one can get!!!!!

But sometimes "happy" doesn't last long.

Consequently, I was a long way from realizing that at this point.

CHAPTER 6

MRS. WALKER

※※

Remember I told you I was four when I was sent to an orphanage in London, Kentucky. When my Mother died, the very last thing she asked her Mother and sisters to do for her was to take care of her six children she was leaving behind, until they could stand on their own two feet. They all meant well, but times were desperate after the war so my family, like most other families were just holding on. The family decided to send us to an orphanage clear on the other side of "Ole Kentucky". It was a sad time for them and us. We were separated into buildings that were named after birds. My new home was called Audubon Hall. We would all sleep in a big clean room that was presided over by a housemother, who had already raised her children. Meet Mrs. Walker, who was a very beautiful older woman. She had long graying. dark hair that she would have a beautician put on top of her head, at the crown, in a basket of tight little curls; the picture of sophistication, intelligence and beauty inside and out. From knowing Mrs. Walker, I was forever drawn to her kind of character, that seemed to make a difference in the lives of anyone she touched. She had a quality that enlarged people's heart, especially little children Therefore, I thought she was the most beautiful lady I had ever seen, plus she was my new Mother...

Everyday, Mrs. Walker would call me aside to stand in front of her until she brushed all of the tangles out of my white, white hair. She would say, "You are just a cotton top, that's what you are, and from now on I'm going to call you, Cotton Top." I think, in a way she spoiled me because I reminded her of her own daughter that was now a school teacher in Louisville. She would go off and see her every once in a while with her little black hat and gloves in the winter and her little white hat and gloves in the summer. Everything always had to match plus she had to smell good too. I saw her many times sprinkle powder under her arms and under her skirt. When she stepped out of her room I always admired her for putting such care into herself. "I think when I grow up I want to be just like Mrs. Walker." When I could barely read, she gave me the duty to read to all the other twenty five girls in our dormitory before our naps and just before bedtime. I loved reading to them, but looking back I realize now that they went to sleep much too soon, but I would just keep on reading until I was tired. One day, when my little friend Charlotte was angry with me for winning jump rope, she yelled real loud that she always pretended she was asleep as she was so tired of those boring script. That was the first time I ever remember being hurt after my mother went home to heaven. I couldn't figure out why she had left us either, but I knew I could trust my Mother. To me, she was the best Mom this side of heaven. She was beautiful too, like Mrs. Walker. Her hair was long and black, her eyes were the prettiest blue I'd ever seen or will see ever again. Well, I lied, my daughter Kristen and her son Colton and my son Joe and John's new daughter Jewel, all inherited those wonderful eyes that people say would light up the sky. Next to Elizabeth Taylor, with her purple blue eyes, I suspect theirs were the most radiant blue I'd ever seen. I had big blue eyes also. I remember when people would come to the orphanage and point their finger at me and say, "We want that one. What's her name? Oh, we love her white hair and big blue eyes." Then the superintendent of the whole school would take me behind closed doors and beg me to go with these people, telling me that they would put me through college, I'd have my own room and someday my own car. "They've already signed an agreement that you will have the best of everything and will be answerable to us here at London School." Now here, "Just say that it is okay to sign you out with them." I would just stand there and start crying and tell them I wanted my brothers and sisters.

I never regretted that big decision that little girl made. That decision brought me to where I am today. I hope to share with you exactly what a little girl knew and wants to share with you. Of course I, the little girl, didn't know I knew it, but I knew I wanted to see my precious, beautiful Mother again and I learned in those scriptures that Mrs. Walker had me read night after night, exactly how to do so. That little girl, named me or named you, learned to some, it's a moment, they know and that's all there is to it, but to some of us we have to journey to it. My journey was to and through my soulmate. I suspect many of you are going my way. I want to try and make it a little easier for you than it was for me. That's the only reason I'm writing such a long letter-story to you. Otherwise, I would have just compacted it into a poem just like any other poet.

I would have sent you this poem, I wrote when I was all grown up and still looking for my other half. In Japan they call it Yang or Ying of your self.

In autumn, I gathered all of my sorrow
And pain and buried them in my garden
When April and spring came to wed the earth
There grew in my garden, beautiful flowers
Unlike, flowers anywhere.
All my neighbors and friends came
And envied me and ask,
"When Summer comes again, Will you not give us seeds
That grew this beautiful garden?"
What could I tell my friends? Yea or Nay!!!!

CHAPTER 7

GRANDMA AND JIM

It takes me back to long ago when one day I was out playing hopscotch on the sidewalk. By now, I was a champion jumper and I guess you could add eater. That's because we played for pennies and when the canteen would open, I made sure, I always had enough for those great big "Babe Ruth's", they used to make. I always would buy a friend one too. Some of those little girls couldn't jump at all. I'd win at table tennis and ruthless at horseshoes. I couldn't be beat at the splits, until one day we found the knife in my inner side foot. I was rushed off to the hospital, then, and a few other times. I finally met my match, when I signed up for baseball. I couldn't get over how fast and tough those girls were on those teams. I decided right then and there not to ever be competitive again.

I loved it when I found out later in college that there was a culture and discipline called, "Tai Chi", that agreed with me and the scriptures that say, "One does not have to compete for what is theirs, it will come to them. Love jumps over waters and moves mountains. It will come to them and will never be taken away. It is frozen in that moment in Heaven, or time, whatever you prefer to call it. Like it or not."

If it's true that every moment is eternity, then eternity is locked into every moment. Sometimes in our lives something happens to drive that home to us. I can't help but think of the millions of cells that come barreling out in the process of making love. I understand that there is enough fertilization to nearly populate the world. So, you can realize how important you are to have been one out of that many that was, let's say, chosen to come here almost randomly picked with purpose. Because, in that process, you're the witness that it never stops.

I sometimes wonder if my grandmother ever understood this or not, or was it just a part of her being. I look back now and marvel at what she accomplished with just a few days of school. She had to clean homes for people when she was just a little girl. She said sometimes it would take her just about the same amount of time to get to the homes as it would to clean it because there were no cars in that area in her day. So my grandmother learned many things from each household. One of the things she cherished and was the most proud of, was to deliver us babies into the world. She was like the midwife in our little town of Haldeman, but that wasn't enough for Alma Hall. She would go to the ladies homes, deliver the babies, bring all their dirty laundry home, boil them outside to make sure they were sanitized in a washtub size black kettle that she made a fire under, then hand scrub each item.

When I think back much of our existence was for those deliveries. My brother Jim would plow up the flat sides of our property and even as far up the hill as he could get. I'd watch him saddle up our old mule, Myrtle, to the huge plow every spring. He'd take his shirt off; sit down on the log he used for chopping grandma's wood; take out his chew; poke some in his mouth and then he would go into what seemed to be deep thought. After a while, he'd be up and running, sweat pouring off of his huge muscles. He'd sometimes beg, "ole Myrtle" to keep going. "Now come on Myrtle, we're almost done with all this gall darn plowing!" I, to this day have never seen my brother angry. I've tried all my life to be more like him. He was almost more like an angel than a man. I have always been grateful that if I had to lose a parent that God placed my brother Jim there for us. I know we need to let him know in some way, how very much we appreciated him. I will.

We did whatever our grandmother said, I think even as little children, we respected her greatly. We would start our gardens by seed after Jim would get the ground ready. All of us took turns keeping the weeds out and the bugs away. I sprayed the cabbage one time with the wrong spray and had to hand wash off every head in the field. I thought I would never eat cabbage again. But I understood it was important to keep trying out in the field as my grandmother would send me to the new mothers' homes and the elderly with a wicker basket full of groceries out of the garden.

Then, I would have to pick up their laundry. She would boil them outside in the wrought iron kettle; rinsing them in bluing water and hang them on the line with the greatest pride. All items matched up, blowing in the wind. She just kept going for other people in our village. I didn't really notice then, but now, I'm in complete awe. I was her little shadow, and sometimes I'd be so tired, I would have rather have cried, but I'd just stand there with that tired little laugh. This is my grandmother's way, my grandmother's idea of fun, I think. She loved it... I sure wasn't going to let her see me cry.

This is what we would do in the summer, when we would get out of the school for orphans. As grandma healed from losing her oldest daughter, my Mother; she realized we were too far away from her for the school year. She decided to have us move to a Christian school nearer home. It was a little missionary school tucked away in the mountains, literally protected from the world.

Our days and classes were always started with prayer and some kind of demonstration of that particular missionary's service. It was a wonderful time for a child, full of exciting good drama from China, Indonesia, the British Isles and Africa and many more places. The missionaries were phenomenal: I couldn't wait to get to my classes. They would always have their souvenirs and monies from that particular region, as they taught one to reach for the stars as they had done. They would beam with pride and they also had the same light in their eyes as Beryl, when they would reminisce about past events and experiences over seas for the Lord and for our country. These were great people. What had I done to deserve such a great honor?

CHAPTER 8

THE PUZZLE OF SOULMATES

On our ride home, Kelsie kept pressing me to go on. "How did you find out you loved him? Are you sure Regennia that he is your soulmate? By the way what is a soul mate?"

I tried in an awkward way to explain what I thought it was. I was soon to learn I hadn't even come close, even though I had found my very own soulmate. I did at least understand that when God made man, he also made a mate for his soul. Yes, there is only one, don't let anyone tell you that there can be several...many loves is not a soul mate. I thank God, even with all the sorrow and pain and great joy, for my soulmate experience. I do realize how different I would have been without it, how very shallow, how on the wrong path I would have been.

I think most people, when they finish working on themselves begin to seek someone out to either verify they have done a good job on themselves or believe that one other person can finish them. It's as though it is a circle. The body draws them near, the brain holds them together as long as they can and the soul finishes them off, either together or separately.

Unfortunately, I was not able to hold on to mine here on this plane. But when I finish this letter-story for you; I hope to have you see that you can hold on to yours forever. It was made for you, it's yours, no one can ever really take it away. It doesn't matter what they do. It's all up to you and the process starts with joy, and then moves into absolute misery and pain, to...can you handle unspeakable joy and the peace that passes understanding that will go on eternally.

Somewhere in there the story began to get ugly. The gold began to get shaken down...

I soon learned that the world moans and groans if you do begin to experience this soulmate process...

CHAPTER 9

ABOUT BERYL

❧❧

About Beryl, I studied him many times when he didn't know I was looking. My heart would want to help him, but I didn't know how to take the pain off his shoulders. His life with Lara had been rocky, I learned she tried to get him into counseling and he would walk out. She knew they needed counseling, when they went to the point of having a gun on one another. I think they were drinking then. He said she was too jealous, but I learned that Beryl loved making a woman feel insecure and jealous. It seemed to make him feel more like a man.

I learned that Beryl had left home at the tender age of thirteen. He said one day that he just hopped on his bicycle and road up the huge mountain pass behind his home in El Paso. His Dad was injured at work and that made his Mother have to go to work to support the family. You can imagine how much he missed her. He realized that, before she got off work, so back down the mountain he came, tired and hungry, and slid in the back door as Maud was coming in the front one. He tried to tell her what he had done, but she just laughed and wouldn't believe him. Later on, I found out that I shouldn't believe him either, but just like Maud, I went on loving him.

So as far as I know Beryl forgot about leaving home until he was thirteen. Then, while his Mom was at work, he went with an older friend and tied one on. He got home late that night; forgot what good Christians his folks were; was staggering all over the kitchen, looking for a late night snack, when his Dad was awakened by the noise. His father came into the kitchen absolutely shocked at his number one son. He yelled, "Beryl, what on earth have you done? This is shameful behavior!!!!"

Beryl said the next day he headed out of there, so embarrassed he could never go home again, that is to stay. He headed up to Silver City to work with the big cowboys on what used to be the Diamond Bar Ranch. He tried hard to keep up with the ole cowboys. One thing they did to test his manhood, even if he had lied about his age, was to send him across that mountain system, for about fifty square miles to deliver salt licks to the cattle and to check for dead ones. .He would be so afraid at night, that he would sit by the fire and sing those songs of his mothers from church. It really didn't chase the critters away at all. What kept him going were the weekends when he would go into El Paso and play as hard as the big boys would.

His mother or his brother doesn't know that one of those wild barbecues turned into a brawl over some other cowboy's sweetheart that was making eyes at little Beryl. The poor guy didn't know that Beryl was just a kid, and came after him with his pocket knife. Beryl still carries some of the scar very close to the jugular vein. Since this never stopped him from going to the bars most of his life, you can guess he still needed extra stimulation to experience life at all. Even finding the Lord seemed more like a contest. He had to out give everyone and out pray and out dress for church. More like a dapper little man than a cowboy.

It didn't matter to Beryl what people thought, not his parents, not Lara and certainly not me. Beryl did just whatever he pleased. He said that even when he was teaching school, he still did just as he pleased. Oh yes, he even got himself through college without high school at all. He earned three teaching degrees with high marks. He was given a position of teaching difficult children at Austin, Texas high school. He would get up in the dark, drive the school bus, teach all day, drive the school bus again, go home set the alarm for a short nap; do that all day, every day. Plus, he was parenting two boys alone as his second wife Dianna had long since left. And in later years, he managed to swing by night. He said he would go home after driving the school bus to and from school, teach all day and make sure the boys were alright, then check the alarm, lay down for a quick nap and up again to dance until midnight. Many times Beryl and Lara won the dancing contests. Lara had made beautiful dresses to dance in. I forget to tell you, she was also a beautiful seamstress. So, naturally pretty soon the worst did happen! One time he was involved with an older woman that he said taught him everything. It wasn't long before that "everything" got him in trouble. The trouble was his first child named Tara. He was fourteen when she came along. The mother was sixteen. They couldn't get along and by the time Tara was born, Beryl wasn't allowed to see her. He told me he went up the fire escape in the El Paso hospital to see her at birth. After that the mother and child moved across the country.

This was the last time Beryl would ever see or hear from his little girl until she was thirty.

Then thirty years later, here came a letter; first, it was delivered to his brother Larry, and he sent it on to Austin. Beryl was beside himself with joy, as he had long since given up on seeing her ever again. He was so exited to hear from his little girl, and he by now had two boys, Shane and Cody, that he had with his second wife, Dianna. I thought Beryl was having a hard time understanding us girls, as he did not have a sister. He also didn't get to raise his own daughter, who he says would have been a lot different, if he had been able to be a guide to her.

CHAPTER 10

ABOUT TARA

❦

My life was running as messy as Beryl's. I always felt that something was missing. I described once how I felt to, that un-named artist and he seemed to understand this haunting feeling that there was something for me that I couldn't find. I remember telling him that I often observed other people that had this hole in their heart also. But, it seemed they padded their heart with education, wealth, and meaningless drama. Anything, that would help them forget the hole. Many turned to addictions of some sort or the other, like shopping, sex, alcohol, dangerous drugs and other destructive behaviors. Kelsie and I pondered hours and hours about that on our coffee breaks and on the phone.

Looking back, I can see I found Beryl; or we found one another so late in life that our hearts were so tattered, that we seemed to punish each other in every way. It was still love alright, the love the bible speaks of saying, "You will be tried like gold." Gold has to go through fire many times to be discovered. It definitely is shaken, just ask any gold miner. We, I must say, grew comfortable with each other's idiosyncrasies, but his daughter grew to resent our union in an impossible way. The hatred she dished out at me became impossible to deal with, that close at hand. She, I suppose, wanted to forget the scriptures that say, "What God has put together, let no man put asunder." I'm sure that means women too. She didn't seem to fear the Lord at all. Instead, she seemed to take great pride in the control she had over her father. Just like Lara had said.

By now Tara was almost fifty. She told me she had been a Wiccan. "What's that?" I asked. She explained that it was the Witches International Corporation of America. I confess, I know nothing about it. I do know I began to be afraid of her, I never knew what she would do or say, except for the letters and phone calls Beryl would allow me to listen to; she would also write him terrible letters about me. I do not know to this day where this hatred came from. I remember, Tara told me one time that she had to live on the streets for a couple of years because she hated her stepmother. She said she would love to actually have a birthday party like everyone else. I delighted for two or three days putting together the best party I could afford. To me it was just like every average American would expect for a party. We had cold cuts, three kinds of salads, potato, macaroni, apple/date, and nuts. We had a beautiful cake with her name on it and plenty of presents to open. What's missing? I don't know, I had never had one either. It seems to me, and of course this is only my opinion, as one can never really know what another person really thinks. She had convinced her Dad that she had become a baptized Christian in a conventional church. At least, that is what he told me. I wonder now that I think back. I was standing outside his and her office that I wasn't allowed to go into; they had the door shut so as I looked down, I could see something bright behind the chair by the door. I was bored so I pulled it out to entertain myself while they did what ever it was they had to do behind those closed doors.

To my shock and horror there was a very expensive, huge book on witchcraft. It had a centerfold of moon changes and how they effect emotion. I was horrified, it reminded me of one of the times my son brought a tee shirt home with "Black Sabbath" on it. It was black with a falling cross of some sort that had fallen into a pool that looked like blood, a large sword seemed to take center stage. What ever it was, my reaction to it was that it was sacrilegious and I had to remove it from our beautiful little house the Lord had given us. My son didn't seem to mind, and to this day, wherever I am, I try to buy them neat shirts. I am so proud of them that they understood that image wasn't a good thing.

By now, I'm wondering why my mate could not see that this was not good. He was a retired teacher with several degrees and could not accept how bad this book was. This was one of our great fights; it was the first time I wanted to leave.

He decided it was time to go over to my house, and as he was backing out of the drive; I mentioned to him what I had found behind the chair. He looked at me, turned several shades of red, his eye brows raised as high as they could, his nostrils flared and he yelled, "You nosey thing! Why don't you mind your own business, you never touch things in some ones home that doesn't belong to you. Do you hear me?" I could never be a victim very well, I knew where I was going, always have always will. I thought.

I took one deep breath, and thought very quickly, I could tell him to stop his car and let me out, slam the door in his face and never look back or I could try to save him, just as I would anyone I cared about. I decided to fight for his soul. I straightened up and screamed as loud as I could, just as I believed his mother would do if she had caught him, "Wilson Beryl Rink what on earth do you have witchcraft material in your house for? Do you know that Witchcraft and Christianity will not mix? Of course you do if you are truly Christian!!!!!!"

He knew I was not going to back down. This was bigger than he or I. Seeing my mind was set, he quieted down and tried to make me believe Tara only used that book for her art work and to paint phases of the moon. He knew that I didn't believe that, so he added, "Well, she'll give up a little bit at a time as she can of her past ways." I told him I believed it didn't work that way. That you either accept your creator's way or you'll try in vain to pave your own. It's then I became afraid for Beryl, and could realize he had a very dark cloud over him and I could begin to realize that I was a part of his Mother's and families prayers. It became a calling to me.

Now here is where I am to blame some what. One, I am nosey about art books. Two, everything in me said, *Run, Don't Walk...Run!* But what did my stubborn self do? I sat there like an idiot. All of my senses screamed at me to separate myself from him and yet my soul held on.

Slowly, it dawned on me that I was in deep trouble. I was going to ask Beryl to let me out of the car at my home where he would come each night with his little over night case, and leave each morning to go live with his daughter across town. When he wasn't with her, she'd be on the phone first thing in the morning and last thing at night. Talk about codependents.

Hello, where was my brain? I'll tell you, I was observing all of this and because I believed that this was my soulmate; I believed I had a burden to push Beryl through his daughters' behavior. I had the belief that I might have been chosen to help Beryl through this, as I had gone through this with my own son and one of his loves. I would say before you seek to help someone lost in this form of rebellion, be sure you can even be in the game; but I can reassure you of this, that if your heart is in the right place, that is if you are sincere about loving the soul that is lost and that includes yourself, all of heaven will cooperate to help. The angels will help and you will become aware of it in little ways. As you became aware of this relationship you won't trade it for anybody or anything in this world, not even your *soulmate.*

CHAPTER 11

ABOUT BERYL AND TARA

❧❧

Now remember, I told you Beryl was not someone I would have chosen, but he continued to hammer at my weaknesses. It felt like fire!!!!! It seemed like if he found out something bothered me, he and his daughter would double or triple whatever it was that hurt, all the while professing how much he loved me and couldn't make it without me. Tara would call and verify those proclamations, by saying, "You just don't realize how crazy my Dad is about you." I think it was their idea of a game. Neither of them had to work, I'm sure they were stark raving bored, but not for long.

Beryl did tell me that he believed, I was or would be his nemesis. I thought, how strange it was to tell someone you were their every thing, even their downfall. I think each of us believed we were in charge of this drama unfolding in front of us.

The strangest part about Beryl, were the signs he insisted on having on all of his vehicles about heaven. The sad part was that it made him believable, which he banked on. If you believed, he honored his signs about heaven and God, then he had you just where he wanted you. Look Out!!!! I warned you, he was not someone I would have chosen as a mate, but God had other plans. I warned you and I was right!!!!

Sadly, everyone in town that knew my husband and would mention him, would always add, "That man with God all over his truck." One of my elderly clients tried to warn me by pointing to his signs on his little green Kia and say, "Remember girl, all that glitters is not gold." I remembered hundreds of times after that. It hit home one time when I overheard him tell my youngest son to just go to church to meet those young pretty girls. "John I tell you, just go to church!!!" John told me later that he couldn't use the Lord like that…But Beryl could.

Beryl could use anyone especially his soulmate. I spent several years caring for him, trying with all my heart to believe in him as my great love. But his and Tara's drama just became worse and worse. Where do you throw in the towel on a mate that heaven itself created for you? I did soon learn. Heavens' time has nothing to do with ours here; until heaven intervenes and until there isn't any doubt at all who is in charge, we seem to blunder on!!!!! My mind goes back to scripture again. I remember it read, "It's not by might, not by power, but by my spirit says the Lord."

The more love you gave these two people, the more punishment they would dish out to you. All it did was send me right back to the scriptures that I had counted on since being sent to that orphanage. I found that everything is there that we need to know, it doesn't matter what the circumstances. It's just hard to believe that something was actually included in the word just for you, just for every circumstance you'll ever need. What a great and wonderful plan. So when all those seeds that might have made it and didn't, we did and also came with wonderful instructions. No one has to wonder about anything, unless they are too stubborn to read and too stubborn to believe. But in the end if you say you want to be with the creator in heaven someday; you will be guided by those scriptures and angels until you're ready to make it on your own.

I wasn't ready yet; I was still bitter that Tara told me that she didn't want an old man around. I guess that she had all she could do to control her Dad. Yet, she wanted my man around all the time and his money. I never witnessed this kind of control on anyone before in my life and I found it very disturbing. I spent most of my time trying to figure out how to get myself and my mate out of this suffocating hold.

I decided the best way was to sell my beautiful home to see if Beryl was really under God and would come with me when I had to leave. It just wouldn't sell, as our Elephant Butte Lake was too low for the tourists that year and we were in the middle of a drought. By having my house on the market, it brought lots of people in my life. They were very honest with me about their feelings toward my husband. They said they felt uneasy around him, as though he was never telling them the truth about himself. I just couldn't accept that he didn't love the Lord ever bit as much as I did and ever bit as much as he seemed to when I first met him with Lara. I also thought he was different because he was born and raised in El Paso, right up town. It wasn't any wonder that he tried to escape there as a child. I admired him for that kind of wisdom, the wisdom of a child. You see we didn't know the truth about ourselves. Does anyone. Yet!!!!!! I knew, at least not to blame him for that.

I'd ask myself why he couldn't see this huge peril and block to his sanity and progression to heaven; the place he promised his mother, he would see her again there. Here's where the work began. He had promised Lara and myself that he would be with us forever in heaven, plus he had a son and father that had already gone home.

Somewhere in here my mind was saying, after losing all these loved ones, I believe Beryl's heart actually broke in pieces. This is the time and opportunity for the daughter to take him over, almost completely, had it not been for the family prayers. As I understand it, Wicca is about control. Remember the book I found and the anger.

The irony to me was, that the very person who had talked his son Shane and his little family into moving out to Virginia, was Tara. Her brother, Shane, wasn't out there very long before Beryl had to make an emergency flight out to Tara's to identify the bodies that were found in the nearby forest. It was labeled a murder/suicide, but Beryl told me it was not true.

I believe something happened right about this time in his life to make Beryl totally vulnerable to Tara. Somewhere in there she took total control of him. Lara thought so and I thought so as well. But did God? Why were they even bothering to bring other people into this? I hope I can show you and I hope she believed she was right. I came to believe that controllers look for someone totally vulnerable, someone they can control, just the way Tara did with her father. There was even questions in our town, if he was her father. It wasn't really anyone's problem or business, except he had me right in the middle of the question. That's pretty bad. It's just as bad a disease as any other form of illness where something other than the health and joy that each of us are given at birth, tries to take over our bodies or someone else's. It is our birthright to live glorious, independent and free. Tell that to a controller. They won't hear you or they will double up on that forceful spirit.

For Beryl and I, this was our greatest challenge and I must add his families. It was very ugly for me to watch and for them. Suffice to say they had talked and talked, they have prayed and prayed and continued to do so as these two continued in their web of deceit, controlled by Tara; the girl whom she says the stepmother couldn't stand her and kicked her out on the streets for a few years. To meet her is to get drawn into the mean street mentality. It just made me realize if you do not have a conscious, your energy is boundless. To save myself, I just had to get out of the way and let God do his work. On both of us.

I learned it's much like rock climbers or bungee jumpers or race car drivers or anyone who needs more stimulation than us ordinary people, who get a kick out of life without all the drama. They do seem to enjoy it. I don't and I hope and pray that you don't get drawn into it as I did, in the name of Love and God.

Beryl and I would breakup, go our separate ways time and time again. He would call and say how very much he missed me and needed to talk. We would meet at a local Dairy Queen, talk for hours about our love for one another and about our differences. Beryl would make up stories to lead me to believe that Tara understood what she was doing and would be just having family dinners with us once a week, after church. I'd believed whatever he said as I had never been around a man with such a dark shadow over him, that would allow him to tell you whatever you wanted to hear, without compunction. I would believe him, but with a watchful eye as a mother would with a newborn child. He and I, in those talks would begin to understand the other and would be blissfully happy as long as Tara could stand it. Then after this beautiful peaceful reunion, the calls and demands on Beryl would start again. Even though I was from a hollow in Kentucky, I knew something was wrong with this picture. We tried to believe it was because we were from separate parts of the country. Me, a hillbilly, from Kentucky and Beryl from the West Texas town of El Paso. However, we were kept so busy by the daughter, we never had a chance to bond, and I finally awakened that it never would happen as long as Tara believed, and relished the thought of being in charge of our lives. She never seemed to realize who was truly in charge. It's a realization we all have to come to sooner or later in our lives…

But then Tara didn't even realize that just as Beryl was telling her everything and seemed to be in her confidence, he was also telling me everything about her. He was allowing me to listen to her phone calls to him, she was yelling at him and crying, because he was with me. He also let me read the letters, horrible letters where she would be calling me names. She would say things to him like this, "Dad you'd better not be around that crazy Regennia, when I'm sending you these computer girls. You seemed to be working harder on that relationship, than the ones I'm sending you!" Then she would quote scripture to back up what ever she was trying to get him to do. She had long forgot the one about "Cleaving and leaving" and "What God has brought together, let no man put asunder." I do believe that Beryl appreciated how very hard I was trying to understand his family. I was trying with all of my heart. The heart with a hole in it. I gave all until there was nothing else to give. Not that love runs out, but the love that goes past the Dad and is stolen by the daughter or anyone else, just simply becomes way too heavy. It's up to each of us individually to estimate when something has gone too far. Don't fail to be fair to yourself. So heavy it was for me, that all I wanted to do was drop it. So drop it I did, over and over again. And through it all I had my friend, Kelsie. That's another bible promise, "You won't be given more than you can handle." So Kelsie and my clients and pretty soon much of our town kept warning me to drop it.

There was a gem in there for me and I hope for you.

CHAPTER 12

THE GEM, THE VILLAGE

Beryl was of German descent and I was a Hillbilly. He loved to remind me of that. He was right. In the hills people live and die for their families, and the ones that had been hand picked to be in their lives. Families all lived close and worked hard in the fields in the summer so that their families and country could eat well. Their tobacco and corn and tomatoes were shipped out at harvest. It was hard in that way, but easier in the spiritual way as we were close to the land and to our loved ones. There was always an older person in each household being taking care of with all the love and respect one can give another. In fact, it was these older ones that when the going got rough, we would always turn to them for their age old wisdom. It was always soothing advice and it always worked. Children would run back and forth to each other's houses, not a care in the world. I could stay over night any where in our little town of Haldeman. One summer our friend, Janet Glover, stayed every night at our house; would get up and eat breakfast with us and go home. Looking back, I now realize why she loved to stay there.

Let me deviate here a little bit and share with you a breakfast at our house in Kentucky. I would awaken to the sound of Grandma kneading out the biscuit dough at her cupboard. She never had to measure, so to this day, I have never seen her biscuits duplicated. They would come out golden brown and elegantly tall, fit for a palace. She would fry sausage and bacon and ham from one of the pigs we slaughtered. The honey in the middle of the table came from her brother, Uncle Marion, who ate all meals with us. Our jams and jellies where made from the fruit us kids would pick as soon as the season hit. There were fields all around us, we'd take our buckets, hats and a stick to hit the snakes away, as they loved the berries also. The sweet milk and butter also came from Uncle Marion's farm. I didn't snap to it then, but I know now that no amount of money could buy those meals. Only love brought them and love bought and paid the price dearly for them and love wore a sun bonnet hat, and her name was Grandma.

I can see now that my Uncle Marion was a lot like Beryl. They both owned a lot of land and that became their main focus. I can remember the state asking my Uncle if he would donate a few inches of road to the state so they could widen and fix up the road to our hollow. He wouldn't give an inch and to this day the road still looks the same. It's a bump and a grind to get to our homes. I felt sorry that my uncle was so cheap, but now I think I'm grateful that he had the fortitude to hold on to what was his and the remote lifestyle he so enjoyed and believed in.

Every other day Grandma would tell me to get in the sugar bowl, as we didn't need banks then, "Take fifty cents and run up to Uncle Marion's to buy a pound of fresh churned butter. I couldn't figure out why we were paying when he always ate at our house. Grandma would act as though she didn't notice her brother's flaws. I suppose that's how we all have to be in the end.

I was a little like that myself, especially when I would get there and Uncle Marion spoke very softly, if he ever spoke at all would ask if I'd like to go with him and Dove, his wife, into the National Forest right in back of their home to check on his cattle. He'd call them by name, and make sure there was salt for them and that all was accounted for. Just like Beryl had done as a child on the Diamond Bar Ranch.

That was the back of Uncle Marion's home, but the front was even more fun. I would skip up to the hill that separated them from the rest of us. On each side of me was a beautiful garden full of wonderful surprises to eat that day. I knew on my way home, they would send me with something from there along with some fresh honey from their beehives. On the other hand, I knew that my grandmother would send me back with some fresh fruit and jams for them. Even at night, when Uncle Marion stayed too long I'd have to walk just behind him so he wouldn't know I was there, to make sure he made it home alright. I couldn't do that now for love or money.

Another thing you would have liked about my grandmother, and it still boggles my mind, was the fact that she never put a delicious home-cooked meal on the table without telling me to go out on the porch to see if anyone was passing by and was hungry. Many people joined us at her table as she was noted as the best cook around…Everything was from scratch. The seeds she had planted, the tilling, the hoeing for weeds and the watchful eye for when it was ready to be prepared for the cellar. That cellar was like a little grocery store and when the family came home, one of their highlights of coming was when Grandma turned them loose in her store. She loaded the cars down with rich naturally grown produce, to be taken to their cities. She also spent her spare time quilting in our living room with the local ladies, making warm quilts for the families so that winter wouldn't be too harsh on them. It always came too fast. I don't know to this day which one came the fastest, winter or Beryl. The women of our village sometimes made our dresses and bloomers from the 100% cotton sacks grandma would save from the self rising flour. I'd like to sit in the corner of the kitchen and hand churn our butter and listen in on their news. It was far more interesting than CNN.

My grandmother took care of her village like no other I have ever seen. She really deserved a medal. One day I'll write you a letter just about her. She was an extraordinary, remarkable person. She knew in her time that it truly did take a village, as President Clinton's wife knew in our time. I'm so glad she wrote about it. I knew in my time it would take a soulmate too and I wasn't about to give up on that belief. I am confident that if I had given up, I might have given up on all beliefs. I held on for dear life and thank God I did…I knew my grandmother would not give up. She always had that great sense, that there was more, always more. I loved her for that, especially that. She always reminded me that "can't" never could do anything!!!!!

The things we learn from our family are invaluable. It was implanted in my mind by my brother, when I was young to be a little skeptical when someone is pulling the wool over your eyes. Jim, my brother, sat down on a huge log by the smoke house and the fence, that sat near the road. It's kind of where my brother and his company would go to tell one another their stories about the night before. I shouldn't have been there, but again, like Tara and Beryl's book, I just happened to catch a glimpse of a round rubber circle in my brother's billfold that he had grabbed out of his back pocket and hurriedly asked me to go down to Moulton's, our store, and buy three Pepsi's and some peanuts. The guys loved to poke the nuts into the Pepsi bottle and drink up. Beryl loved to do that too. I asked Jim what on earth that rubber circle was tucked into one of the slots of his billfold? He and LeRoy grinned at one another. "Why," he said, "that was a drinking tube for when he stood outside the country church windows and flirted with the girls on the inside, he wouldn't have to worry about tearing away from his drink." He said, "in his pocket, was a small bottle of water or you could guess whiskey, so that if he got interested in a pretty young thing; he wouldn't have to leave for anything." The girls loved Jimmy; he had those same beautiful sky blue eyes, full of the innocent mischief of a teenager. The guys just threw their head back with laughter and then kind of doubled up and that laughter turned into a laughing brawl until tears ran down their cheeks. After Jim married and left home, I found that unwrapped circle, by the old woodpile with his chew cans. I surmised that something was wrong with that story, and I surmised something was wrong with Beryl's also…You see, I'd had plenty of practice through my brother and his horse shoeing friends.

Granted sometimes you can't catch lies; sometimes you don't even want to, especially if you love the liar. Or is it love if it's lies? Or could it be something that drives one into a destination that they have no idea where they are going. They will!!!!!

I believe there comes a time in everyone's life when they hit a crossroad. I mean HIT!!!!

CHAPTER 13

THE CROSSROAD

Well my time had not come yet, and I kept blundering on. I was totally in there with my soulmate, lock, stock and barrel as they say. I just couldn't register that when Beryl would ask me to marry him, all four times, that each and every time, I had to go through Tara for everything concerning he and I. Even with all I had to learn and the painful experiences; I would not change a thing as I look back now. Looking forward, I would have changed everything if it had been in my power to do so, except for the wonderful prayers and bible reading fellowships we had together. It was always a happy time and happy memories for me to visit Beryl's brother's family still living in El Paso not far from where they were raised. You could have guessed, I would have changed everything that shook and rattled me and tried me like fire. I didn't like it! But above all, I didn't want to miss heaven. That's what I had told my heavenly father.

I do believe if we tell God, we want to be in his home eternally, we must be willing to tolerate the test he sends to prepare us and show us the way. I believe we are actually prepared for heaven and we show God that we can be trusted there. I believe also that a marriage is like that. It's the same kind of commitment, a kind of practice run. How are you doing??????

Beryl and I didn't do well at all. Remember the golden essence I told you about with the appearance of what seemed like an angel. That sweet bolt of light or energy or both shot through me and I was energized; that same memory or energy comforts me today. Years later, I think it brought with it knowledge and trust of another world, of eternity and the kingdom to come; because the pool of golden essence was bubbling, but there was no need of oxygen that could get through the golden swells that were trying to make a bubble. I told you, I would go everyday to my little knotty pine beauty shop in the Paradise Mountains and hope I would experience that eternal moment again.

After studying several religions, I realized it was a moment; but also a lifetime all wrapped into one. I understand the visit was God's reply to my seeking him and in my time of need he gave me this awareness to help me raise the three children that he put there in my charge. I think often was it God's glory. Yes! And he placed a man there saying in a way, "Come on, you can do it." The mystery of it also said, "I have so much more to teach you, if you want to live in my kingdom of peace. I've promised that there will be no more problems in heaven, so with your gift of free will, you are telling me if you can do it or not. I placed information everywhere for you, but I won't force or coerce you. If you want to live in my kingdom, rest assured, I am helping and guiding you. I am allowing you to get a glimpse because you have the courage to tell people. Also you are very vulnerable and fragile, so they will listen."

In a way, it was like a heavenly baptism as I began to realize it had endowed me with the strength to follow through with courage the decisions I had made for heaven and would be making for heaven, especially my soulmate quest. What an honor! It's there for everyone. We are told, "Knock and he will enter. Seek and you will find." It's more rewarding than anything money could buy. It's free for the asking…can you imagine?

I'll tell you again, money cannot buy this experience. It's absolutely free. It only takes our decision to want it sincerely, and you will be made aware that you are being guided along wonderfully. And if you are lucky you may even get a glimpse of heaven as I did.

I'm not bragging, please don't take it that way. I say often to my father in heaven, if my mother had to go home early, I'm so grateful you allowed the missionaries to teach and guide me toward you. I know it's not free until you pass it on.

Just by sitting quietly and listening, many things will come to you in the stillness. Have you ever noticed how busy and noisy the world is now? Have you ever noticed how many people are medicating themselves just to quiet the soul down? Hippies did have this going for them in the 70's. It seemed they could understand the direction the world was going in and tried to get people to understand that in the end after everything is tried, it is still just the brain doing the function and there's a natural God given way to make it perform for you, by seeking out rest, relaxation in a peaceful environment. Then all the gifts of heaven will come to you without crazy side effects. Life then takes on a new meaning. You will, or at least I did, will only want pure and true events in your life. You will have the strength and courage to reach out and help others, and you'll be able to recognize deceit and try to change it.

CHAPTER 14

THE SEARCH

๛

The way I found out was very painful. I recognized Beryl through our long conversations as the soulmate that I had been searching for all my life. From my college courses, I remember studying Freud's theory, that by five, the child is the parent of the child. Meaning they now should have life skills of reasoning developed enough to see them through life's challenges. It was about this time for me that it began to dawn on me, that there was more of me. I began to feel incomplete. I became aware that there was a huge hole in my heart, that nothing else could fill except by that man God intended for us to be helpmates. In the Bible we are told that when God made man, he put him to sleep and took a rib to make him a mate. This awakening in my spirit, led me to tell my family that when I grew up, I was going to marry a preacher; (Beryl was trying to get ordained, by his Uncle for prison ministry.) They would just laugh at me and say, of course you are, and we are going to climb Mount Everest. I would wonder why they didn't believe me, I was that positive.

We're so spoiled, God's children are and we're all his. We assume a soulmate will be just a perfect and glorious affair, and maybe for a few it is. I believe if you tell God that you don't want to miss heaven, he, in his great capacity to love will send you the conditions that will guarantee with his help that you will not miss your heavenly home.

My journey or process to heaven and my soulmate was not easy, which meant that Beryl's was not either. Beryl and I would come as close as two people could get, almost one. It seemed to enrage Tara, and she would do everything she could to split us up, in other words put asunder.

One of her favorite tricks was to have her father post sale signs all over town for my beauty shop for three years, so they could have more time together during the day. They worked together by day and he would come at night with a travel bag; tried to sleep and leave after breakfast in the morning. He told me he was doing that because I wouldn't give him the house. I do remember offering to let him buy in when we got married. I had already paid two thirds of it off. I told him he could be half owner of it, if he would pay off the other third. "No I don't think I'd better do that." He said. I told him that was okay, let's just divide up the utilities. Which ones do you want to help with? He informed me that it wouldn't be fair to him to pay anything, if I didn't give him the house like a good Christian should. "You're supposed to submit to me remember?"

He moved into my house without asking and that was only half moved in, so I told my beloved soulmate, perhaps he had made a mistake. I told him to go back home until he was sure he wanted to be with me. I was nice that time because we truly had the most beautiful month of my life and it didn't cost anything...yet!!!!! It was great I believe, because we were inseparable and one. We were scriptural. All of heaven had opened up to us.

Beryl had a plan and God had a plan. I thought back after our marriage at the courthouse, how Beryl was pushing me to hurry home to consummate the marriage. I asked him, "I think we're supposed to feed the witnesses. Would that be alright?" He was still very pleasant and kind to me and agreed. His daughter and her adopted daughter had already gone home. He called them to come and meet us also at the restaurant. From that day forward, we could never eat out without them. It began to feel more and more like a front to me. I began to try to balance our family out to a normal all American family. It just wasn't to be.

Consequently, my soul mate was full of deceit that he had learned as a child on the streets, so to speak, and so did his daughter, as that's where they both were as children. In that way, they were experiencing life, one quart too low of the love they should have had if they had decided to stay where they were. Too young, they didn't have the warm guidance and assurance that a child should have. They were seriously lacking in the skills that would bring them first, this temporary relationship with a soulmate here on this plane called earth and then a relationship in heaven where unrest will never be capable of setting up again. All of our actions, I believe, here on earth is really just to tell God if you want to be in that haven of rest he has waiting for us, even a mansion with our names, each of our names on it, we are told, will be there too. But all negativity has to be washed out of our hearts, minds and souls. Every flaw that we have, we must be willing to give up. Why? Because we are shown through scripture that war cannot ever enter heaven again. I'm purposely not giving scripture, as you will be given it from a higher power than myself....Just ask your heavenly Father.

It's never about what I do, but what has been done for us and is continually being done on earth and in heaven. When we contact heaven with conversation, called prayer, he listens and listens well!!!! You begin to see changes in your life, and you begin to love it.

Beryl could pray beautiful prayers, I never heard his daughter pray, but I know she said she did. It always seemed to me that their prayers must be one sided conversations with God. I wondered if they ever reached heaven as prayers are supposed to do, because of the pain they were bringing to peoples lives. The Lord taught me that even the people who pray and don't lead exemplary lives, even their prayers are used for God's purposes.

CHAPTER 15

DICHOTOMY

𓆩𓆪

Beryl was such a dichotomy, it was interesting to observe the distinct differences he had. On one hand he would write out big checks to missionaries for what ever their needs were; I met with some of the missionaries in a restaurant one morning for breakfast and she told me that Beryl supported them lucratively. Beryl drove me around New Mexico and Texas showing me all the signs he had paid for. I think it was six thousand twice a year for one and he had several. I saw him give his grandchildren loans of fifteen to twenty thousand dollars. But on the other hand, when it came to us, he absolutely didn't like taking care of us. I ordered a Whopper and fries and a milkshake, one time, at you can guess where, and Beryl told the hostess to change that order to the ninety cent burger. She thought it was the funniest thing she'd ever heard. I told her, he wasn't kidding and she looked shocked at me, like; *What on earth are you doing with that man?*

I thought I knew what I was doing with Beryl, but life kept telling me in one way or another that I really didn't comprehend the height and depth of where we were going. It bothered me a lot that he didn't buy decent food to go into his own body. Nothing was making sense anymore. Wasn't a soulmate supposed to be fun? We just wanted out; we just couldn't see eye to eye. I was believing that our love for one another should be like God's love. Little did we realize, it was; he just wasn't finished with us yet. Now it makes sense many moons later. I read in those scriptures that we would be tried like gold in the fire, rattled, shaken and separated out of the debris, that attaches it's self to gold. Little did I realize it meant, even me....even Beryl. I often times thought I was the gold and he was the debris. He would just as often, think he was the gold and I was the debris. In reality we both were shattered broken pieces.

Thank goodness God has a sense of humor! One time he had Beryl's retired cousin show up in our town. They were from Arkansas and had come to Truth or Consequences to literally go gold panning with us. By now, I couldn't even handle that, as it seemed he couldn't keep his hands off of her. Of course they had known one another for years, but Satan saw the perfect opportunity to get his wedge in. I couldn't believe this man of God could be so insensitive. Why didn't he just take a hammer and hit me over the head! They didn't know I knew a different Beryl. A Beryl that was completely indifferent to me. Satan reminded me about what Lara had shared with me a few times. She was upset at Beryl for buying his daughter a new car when she had to drive one ten years old. But that was a lot better than he did for me. My car broke down and he let me walk all over town for several months. Oh, I could call him and beg him or his daughter to come and pick me up. But I was much too proud for that...I was in too deep!!!!!

I did the right thing. I began to ask every one I met, for prayer for mine and Beryl's situation. And that was the catch, you cannot call it prayer if you do not have the belief to back it up. You cannot call it love if you do not have the same care or greater care for your loved one than for yourself. You cannot call it a soul mate, unless it does the work on your soul to get you to die to your ego daily.

The stress became so great with Beryl and his daughter that I, through prayer, decided to sell that beloved home to see if he would finally leave and cleave with me or stay with his daughter. I loved my home with all of my heart and I felt privileged to be able to hang on to it as we were going through a drought in New Mexico. It just would not sell; people would fall in love with the home and put down deposits and it still wouldn't go through. Beryl tried as hard as I did to sell the home. In his frustration one day, he yelled at me again. "You didn't give me the house, so you can pay the bills. It's not my problem!!!!" By now, I realized that I was in the middle of a nightmare, not a wonderful dream coming true.

It was okay though, I remember telling God whatever it took, I wanted to have my mansion with my name on it. Beryl was the only one helping me to claim it. We didn't know that at that time, so we continued to love one another desperately and to function fruitlessly.

CHAPTER 16

OUR WORST FIGHT

🕊🕊

I suppose our worst fight was over him being married to me, and living with his daughter day after day. He'd come at night with his travel bag and because the house wouldn't sell, this went on a few years. He seemed to want the amenities of a marriage but not the burdens. I'd look at him and think; It's only a burden because you're making it one. He just couldn't seem to make that leap to God and then the tiny step to me becoming one.

One of the dumbest things we disagreed about; he would come over in the evenings after a hard day in the Beauty Shop and want a hot meal on the table and his feet or back rubbed. As I was rubbing his back, I told him we had a ninety two dollar bill with the gas company to pay, or they would turn off the gas in the morning. He told me he couldn't help and added that I should call my son Joe and see if he would help; although he knew he wouldn't. When he said that; he then sat up quickly, no longer enjoying the back rub and laughed at my predicament.

I was so embarrassed to have to call my son as I knew he wasn't getting regular pay as the ranch gave him a place to stay and they bartered the rest. But the next thing I knew I was hearing, "Sure Mom. I'll send it over by Shortie." I have to tell you about Shortie. He grew up with my son in Socorro, New Mexico. They went to school together and his brother was a local policeman. Well, in one of our fights, and Beryl never knew this until he reads this story, that these guys were having a drink of some sort with Joe when I called. My phone didn't hang up; all the men heard how he was yelling at me and that put them all on edge with him from then on. They didn't give a quarter about understanding him.

So by that incident they knew it wasn't easy for me. It was about ten o'clock at night, when we heard a knock on the door. Beryl and I were getting ready to go to bed and was quite surprised. I yelled, through our thick metal white door, "Who is it?" "It's me, Shortie, Joe sent me over and I have a hundred dollars for you." I was so grateful, but it only made Beryl furious. He began to pack up his little overnight kit, when I saw that, I lost it every time he couldn't even spend the night with me; he'd find any excuse to go to his daughters. I helped him, by throwing all of his toiletries, all of his grooming aids outside all over the front porch, something broke, which made me realize the shock I was in over his attitude. I couldn't win!!!!! I forgot to tell you, he had me baby sit his little dog Sweet Pea, who I loved for a couple of weeks while he went to Tucson to visit his grandson Lane. Beryl did at least try to stand in for his son's denial of the cutest and smartest grandboy ever!!!!!!! Beryl just told me to work hard in the shop and he would see me in a couple of weeks. But; here we go again, there was another reason he liked to go to Tucson. "Hello, Regennia!!!!!!"

It set up such a disturbance in our marriage and I learned later in Lara's also. I believe Beryl's worst weakness, is not understanding women at all. I'm sure Janine, realized her interference was hurting me. One time she came and spent a week in my husband's home he had with Tara during the day. I actually had to go to dinner with Beryl, Janine and Tara. I kept making excuses for them. My number one goal was to express God and his kingdom, and that will always be first, but I wasn't good at it as I didn't comprehend what was really happening. Yet!!!!!

About three years rolled around and on one level Beryl and I drew close, really close. Even with all the stresses and problems, but always the street mentality was operating in our relationship. I didn't understand it then, but hoped to explain what I learned, and now why I am so grateful for the relationship.

I believed Beryl loved me as much as he could love someone. Well, maybe more than his internet women, that Tara would choose for him and insist he stay away from me. She wanted him to work on what she sent him to love. She didn't realize that I could hear all of the conversations, some of them were so heated about staying away from me, his wife, that I could hear her all the way across the room. He let me read the mean letters she would write about staying away from me. I do not understand where all this hatred came from. Her Dad said that I had called her a witch. I was shocked about the witch part, but it unnerved me that she was a Christian and would believe gossip. Had she come to me and asked, I would have told her that I didn't even know what a witch was. To tell the truth, after writing her a long letter pleading with her to let her father and I bond; she doubled up on her calls and things for Dad to do, and by him writing us off, I did think she was something I never understood. As I understood it the rift was never from me, but from the God, he preached about and carried all over his vehicles.

That's all over now. We're all healed. And I'm sorry that we all hurt one another's feelings in the name of love and in the name of God. But think of the beauty, we were actually going somewhere.!!!!!! Hang in there it get's better!!!!!!

CHAPTER 17

WE'RE ALL HEALED NOW

It seemed to me that Beryl and Tara truly believed they were in charge. I knew the day would come when the Lord would intervene and all of us would know it was the Lord, because it would be conditions only he could bring about. Then we could not "deny," "deny," "deny," in anyway.

Well after four attempts at our marriage, the Lord finally did say, "Enough is enough and too much is nasty." He and his angels produced a moment that made Beryl and a computer woman, his friend Hal, and my best friend Kelsie and myself sit up and take notice. It was the same God that parted the waters for Israel. The same God that made Joseph to rule over his brothers that had sold him into slavery; then he eventually ruled over all of Egypt when he gave him the vision to interpret the King's dreams. I want Beryl and Tara to think about this, that if that heathen king had not the wisdom to listen to one of God's own, where would we be now? Dreams are important!!!!!

I love singing that ole gospel tune—*Joshua fought the battle of Jericho and the walls came tumbling down*. And do you know how he fought the strongest army around? He fought just as God had said with prayer and trumpets. Is it frozen still in time? Yes!!!!! Could you or I or any one you know here, do that? No! Can God do that? Well, it's our history. You fill in the rest.

Ours was not traumatic in that way, but in another it was. It happened like this:

By now, you might have guessed it was another day, another year, another lunch break with my good friend Kelsie. Do you remember her? By now we had gone to lunch or breakfast day after day, that was by now beginning to turn into year after year, and with that were the discussions about our soulmates. Kelsie would ask prying questions about who they are, where do they come from and how do you find your own?

Here's the answer that Kelsie helped me uncover, after years and years of searching.

It is the person that God made for you to do work on your own soul. Remember too, the Lord said to Adam. "I will make for you a helpmate." God left it open there, but he did add that he had taken a rib of Adam's to produce Eve for him. Now we know scientifically that is not possible. Only with God it is!!!!

To Kelsie and I, we figured that rib could mean, blood of our blood and bone of our bones, in short our ancestors. You can imagine how proud I was when Beryl's mother's brother, a preacher agreed that he realized that Beryl and I were made for each other. He would add with laughter, "So you all should stop being so mean." You see, it's the prayers that went to heaven all along for us; it means red flags along the way that give you clues about a person, but above all, it means and this is the point of this long story to you; it's the work we need to do on our own souls.

CHAPTER 18

A LESSON TO LEARN

❦

We were probably at our meanest point, just the way a firecracker fizzes and spurts just before it goes out. That's the way we were in our story even though it's true, went out. Oh! Wait a minute, that's what I thought would happen, but it was just the complete opposite of that. I'll tell you why!!!!!

It's a hard lesson to learn, but Kelsie and I learned it well. She had ordered a crispy chicken salad and I a hot fudge sundae leisurely. It was like we owned the world. Kelsie even said, "I wonder what the rich are doing now?" We laughed over the dumbest things, it didn't take much to make us happy.

Leisurely, we sauntered around in the dairy queen and laughed and talked with people we didn't get to see every day, because her husband/boyfriend was working in Albuquerque and my soulmate, the love of my life, had just called and said he was sorry that he couldn't be there when I was so sick, but he was in Oklahoma closing a deal on a nut farm he owned. I knew some guy had bought him out, called from time to time, saying he couldn't make a payment; so it all made sense to me. Beryl told me how much he loved me and to get ready for Poverty Creek, his mountain retreat, that we would go there in a few days. By now, I was totally at peace, no matter what Beryl did or said. That's what prayer does.

We talked and we giggled a while longer, people were always accusing us of having too much fun. Then we decided to go by the fruit and vegetable stand for our family's dinner. Nonchalantly we walked to her little blue Cavalier. We always knew hers as it had a huge dent in the side, where another woman popped us in one of those grocery store parking lots. It should have killed us, but a young man was going in front of us, could see what she was doing and just laid on his horn. That's all that saved us as she was in her boyfriends old huge Dodge. That was a hard blow, but Beryl dealt one harder just a little later as we headed down Date Street.

Kelsie goes, "Oh, there goes Beryl." I reassured her it wasn't, that I had just talked with him and he's closing a deal in Oklahoma. Kelsie insisted, "No Regennia, I know that was Beryl, because he had the GOD signs all over his truck and fifth wheel!" I argued with her that just couldn't be him. "Okay, let's see! She jerked the little blue Cavalier around so fast, that it made my head swim. As the car straightened out, my mind went into high gear. *My goodness, she's right!* There's his fifth wheel with Jesus and his out stretched hands that Beryl had hired an artist to paint on the back with the words above Jesus' head that said, *See I won't forget you.*

So, here we were several years later and Kelsie, reached over again, kind of took my arm and shook it as if to awaken me from a dream, she's yelling again just like she did before, "Isn't that him Regennia? Let's just see where he's going!"

My mind was racing now, things he'd said, things I'd answer back to him, with thoughts like, "All of creation is coupling, a bringing together the parts to the whole and where so ever, I look, I behold you and the secrets of life is reflected in your eyes." Sometimes Beryl would smile and say, "Is that scriptural?" and then give me a deep warm, teasing kiss. It was the close times to him, that made me feel the closest to God and I'd wonder if he felt the same; how could he not when someone had waited all their life for him, and God's work!!!!!!

"He put his turn signal on to turn into McDonald's." Kelsie said, "Oh good, you can get a good look at who he's with and let her have it." That's what Kelsie would have done. He pulled over and parked on the side as though he was waiting for someone else. So Kelsie looped around and parked right to the side of him. We saw a dark headed lady pop up; she turned and looked at us in a stunned manner. Then came Beryl's face looking me right in the eyes. I was wondering why she was in my seat, but Kelsie and I, simultaneously were frozen in time; we couldn't move; we couldn't speak. But still a small voice seemed to say, "See, Beryl doesn't even recognize you Regennia the soulmate, I made for him." That's what it will be like, when each person's probation is up. There's Christ; there's Satan, which one do you know, love and follow. I knew that Christ had said that my sheep know my voice and will follow me. That was the most clear warning anyone could have.

I don't believe Beryl had ever been caught in his deceit before...

Picture it like this. It was a time freeze where you could actually witness God removing his grace from us. It was a terrible thing!!!!! I realized then and there that one cannot keep asking God for help and keep the prayers going up to heaven; that God in all his mercy cannot keep from responding.

But responding in a way that will ransom you out of Satan's charm and in a way that will guarantee you will make it home to him in the same manner a loving parent watches over the care of their family. You never stop wanting the family to come home and home is just an airport or station to heaven.

In that moment, frozen forever in eternity, we were aghast at this man who had God and heaven written all over his vehicles, the irony was that he wasn't even close. For a while I thought he was, I hoped he was, especially me, being his soulmate. But God knew that neither one of us, or maybe all of us, were not ready for his kingdom. But I came to realize and understand this, that what God has given you to do—He will eternalize it in his kingdom for ever and ever.

Never let Satan convince you that something was taken away from you and that he is in charge.!!!! God produced that moment to show all of us that, what is ours....is frozen in eternity. Once you get a glimpse of this gift to us, you will never let Satan convince you that he is in charge with his money, his beauty, his clout. It is simply God's...

It is all his! Our role is to simply say yes, we want to be with him forever and he will bring about the conditions for you to make it home...

You will find yourself being grateful for everything; yes! even the hardships and heartaches. I know you have met people in your lifetime that you wonder what on earth keeps them going?

The whole point of this story to you is to simply say that it is God in you, in us forever.

Again, remember all things are eternalized, you cannot loose what is yours, it's impossible, just try and loose the sky. It can't be done.

So my dearly beloved soulmate, Wilson Beryl Rink, ironically again was producing a movie called, "Hell's Rage", and it seemed to me that he was making a movie about hell and was well on his way to hell with lies, deceit and greed. But he knew and I knew, that prayer changes everything. We come with a guarantee, we'll be alright just for the asking. Do you know any better gift than that?

And always rest assured that what is your is eternalized forever. You are a winner! A great winner at that!!!!! When you are in search for your soulmate, just always make sure your heart is centered with Christ and His Love and you will find your own Jewel's of great price. Someday, I will ask you for your autograph when we really succeed and remember, as my soul sister Dolly Parton sings, God will always love you and in a way, I will always love my Soulmate Warrior.

Your Friend, with a full heart and running over, Regennia

Respectfully edited by, Wilsie Beryl Rink